This Unexpected Life

Poems by Brenda Linkeman

Spartan
Press

Spartan Press
Kansas City, MO
spartanpress@gmail.com

Spartan
Press

Acknowledgments:

The author would like to thank the editors of the following publications where some of these poems first appeared (in some form or another):

"THE MARINE" (published in the *Trailer Park Quarterly,* 2022), "MOIRAI" (first published in *Strange Gods of the Prairie, The Gasconade Review,* 2021), "QUINTESSENCE" (first published in *Strange Gods of the Prairie, The Gasconade Review,* 2021), "THE FARM" (first published in *Strange Gods of the Prairie, The Gasconade Review,* 2021)

I would first like to thank Mark McClane, president of the Osage Arts Community, in Belle, Missouri. Mark recognizes creative people, and instinctively knows how and when to give gentle nudges of encouragement. I would also like to thank Jason Ryberg, Spartan Press, who opened the door for me to publish. I want to express my appreciation to John Dorsey, who organizes poetry events at Barb's Books in Belle, and, where I participated in my first Open Mic. Angela Ruskiewicz and Harold Brown both read through earlier selections of poems, some of which made it into this book. Elizabeth McCartney and Rebecca Sidwell both gave me encouraging feedback. I am thankful to Adam Maness, and the 442s of St. Louis, for composing and playing incredible jazz, that not only inspires my art, but my poetry, as well. "Penny" and "Martha" taught me valuable lessons that I have carried with me through life. In particular, "Martha" reinforced that art and play are powerful tools a child uses to communicate. A sincere thank you to Tom Elmore, who illustrated the title page image for this book. And, last, I want to thank all of my Facebook friends and relatives who have "liked" or "loved" various poems, and who have been a huge source of encouragement for me.

Table of Contents

this america

Wanda, Illinois / 1

Things You Couldn't Believe / 3

Optimistic High / 4

The Greatest Generation / 5

The Farm / 6

The Camelot Years / 7

High Heels / 8

The Echo of Bison / 9

Seeing Into Souls / 10

Cold War Couples / 11

Nine Eleven / 12

The Marine / 14

The Chocolate Poodle / 15

The Fountain / 16

The Serbian Clergyman / 17

Penny / 18

Miles to Go / 20

It's 4:50 at the DMV / 21

The Dollar General / 23

The Dog / 24

Connected Like Clockwork / 25

We Are One / 26

Masks / 27

The Quiet Zone / 28

memories (1962 – 1971)

The Segregated Town / 31

The Bay of Pigs / 33

November 1963 / 34

Rufus Youngblood / 36

Crazy Martha / 37

The Boy and the Parakeet / 38

The Quarter / 39

Retaliation / 40

The Football / 42

The Girl's Locker Room / 44

Falling Rocks / 45

Boeing 747 / 46

Nixon / 47

staying centered

Moon's Glow / 51

Zephyr / 52

A Calm Soul / 53

Spatial Lapse / 54

The Speed of Light / 55

Continuous Flow / 56

Perspective / 57

Moirai / 58

Sea Wind / 59

Circles / 60

Progression / 61

Pen to Paper / 62

A Poem Appears / 63

In Your Soul / 64

For Richard / 65

Suppose / 66

Close to Me / 67

Quintessence / 68

Watching the Stars / 69

Vines / 70

Misplaced Cares / 71

Order / 72

Hijinks / 73

Does It Matter / 74

Finally / 75

Emily / 76

The Fragrance of Memory / 77

My poetry reflects on memories of unexpected life events. Unexpected life events are continual and will occur across the lifespan. They are unanticipated surprises that you did not imagine would happen, events you did not plan for, sometimes funny, sometimes life changing. Interspersed among memories, whether positive or negative, are the quiet, reflective moments that create balance in our life.

-Brenda Linkeman

I use memories, but I will not allow memories to use me.

-Deepak Chopra

This collection of poetry is dedicated to my parents,
who always gave me space to grow.

this
america

WANDA, ILLINOIS

the cottage was small and white and quiet
tall windows on the back porch let in bright light
shelves were lined with various sized potted African violets
royal purple, with tiny yellow centers, and dark juniper
    green leaves
the now fallow field on the side of the house
was used as a truck patch, growing sweet watermelon and
    cantaloupe

she met us at the door leading to her small kitchen
wearing a smooth, printed cotton dress, with a half-apron
made of similar fabric wrapped around her waist
and tied in the back

he sat heavily in a faded easy chair smoking a cigar
resting his elbow on the arm of the chair
smiling with his eyes

aunts and uncles and cousins soon began to trickle in
we ate roast beef and hot mashed potatoes
cousins played red rover, charades, tag, or card games
staying up as late as we could, laughing, and making too
    much noise

later they all would load into their cars and leave
and for a few moments it felt too quiet
we stayed

someone pulled the attic stairs down from the hall ceiling
it was a wonder that an entire room was up there
the rickety stairs slid down, a section at a time
until they hit the hard wood floor
beds of various sizes filled the room
the sheets and blankets were fresh and cold
we slept soundly
the next morning we had fried eggs and bacon

but we never ate melons
I wish we had

THINGS YOU COULDN'T BELIEVE

(memories from a WWII Army Veteran)

"I saw things you couldn't believe"
dead horses
tanks
trucks
and wagons
broken down on the road
this Frenchman found a plane in '44
and he flew it out
we saw planes all over
twenty-four hours a day
we slept in foxholes
ate c-rations
and k-rations
we ate out of cans
and lived on the ground
we never had it too bad
we were under Patton
and he was on the move!

OPTIMISTIC HIGH

he was a confident man when he first met her
but it had not been so when he was younger

raised on a melon farm
he had been taught to milk cows
on Sundays he ate roast beef and mashed potatoes
but during the Great Depression he learned to eat pork

thick black hair
tall and lanky
he was an awkward teenager
he felt homely back then
now he stood tall and confident

she was a beauty
with a sparkling intellect

the two were drawn to each other in a powerful way
it was much more than physical attraction
sensing perhaps a certain destiny before them

after the second World War
there was a pervasive sense of euphoria
that gave everyone an optimistic high

they married
she had red hair

THE GREATEST GENERATION

I doubt my father ever drank a latte

computers were the size of a small room

Old Spice, pencil shavings,
and "Heerrre's, Johnnie!!!"

he did own a microwave
but I never saw him use it

no crocheted afghans
or cushiony toilet seats

politics were argued face to face
and not behind pixels

senior trips to the city,
tomatoes, newspapers, and
crippled hands that gripped a golf club

my father took his coffee black

THE FARM

(Campbell County South Dakota)

The still, spacious kitchen at the farm,
before the room filled with bright, bright sunlight.
Voices before the gathering of belly warmed chicken eggs,
and bowls of cereal,
and warm, fruity kuchens.
The small, top drawer filled with pennies,
and nickels, and dimes.
It smelled of gum, minty and sweet.
The floor in the utility room is cool.
The stone shaped tiles fit together
like a large sepia shaded puzzle.
I imagined the shapes were countries,
or boots, or spaces to play hopscotch on.
The floor was strong, and its integrity
lasted long after the farm was abandoned.

THE CAMELOT YEARS

mother drank milk
out of those waxed cartons
leaving red lipstick kisses

Hamburger Helper, drive-in theatres,
cold cream, bobby pins, and perms

cigarettes were fashionable

my cousins were fascinated
with her makeup rituals
hanging on the edge of the sink counter
watching each step
involving those small tubes and jars

Sunday hats, Jell-o molds,
station wagons, and Della Reese

she never had to work
dad took care of the crabgrass
she took care of braces, glasses,
and Dr. Seuss

HIGH HEELS

mother wore high heels to the beach
I don't know how she did that
we collected some seashells
ate lobster
and had coffee at Café du Monde

THE ECHO OF BISON

our red head mother died

the viewing
was in a small chapel
near a Missouri River bridge
watched over by a stone statue
of Sitting Bull

she was buried deep
in Dakota prairie land

"why is mommy so cold?"

gramma wailed an ancestral cry
and the echo of bison stampeding
over my mother's grave
pounded in our heads

SEEING INTO SOULS

when she was born
her parents looked down
on their small infant

something about the baby overwhelmed them
and yet, drew them near to her

they huddled close
arms entwined
gazing down on the baby
her eyes were not yet focused
but she looked through them

they wondered if other babies
could see into souls

COLD WAR COUPLES

undisclosed
this resolute
optimistic playful space
where magnified causes
lost their point
and the debate
continued to weigh down logic

where Barbie flirts with Ken
who is not really a GI Joe
and Barbie
only dreamed of being Barbie
so instead they revealed
they were not
Dick and Jane of course
but maybe Nancy
and one of those Hardy boys
locked in the pages
of many children's ideas
and aspirations
and where their children
played with Potato Head
hula hoops and Slinkys
who thought it was hot outside
and that the grass was green
but it was really
just a cold, cold war
of saber thrashing words

NINE ELEVEN

(inspired by the jazz group The 442s - Phender's Pholk Song)

eyes reaching
reaching from dark spaces
running from thick clouds
emerging into light
but it's not light
it's a darkness not defined by color
a darkness with no space

life falling
step lightly
breath slowly
sense the pulse
the slow energy
the thick cascade of fear
dancers spinning in slow motion
with open palms pleading

spinning a little faster
confusion and uncertainty
sustained by steps
by slow steps
heat
panic
dizziness
sleeplessness
the hole in your heart

the rock on your head
the dirt on the ground

that spinning again
just be with people
don't be alone

THE MARINE

it was a silent walk
through the Art Deco District on South Beach
the breeze was mild and warm
few businesses were open
the hurricane left a dank smell
I thought he was kidding
when he asked,
"Do you want to get a tattoo?"
his face was alive with anticipation
but I said, "No, that's ok."
tattoos are like roadmaps to Marines
after that he seemed lost as to what to say
the empty streets led to
the beachfront
a flattened beachball
seaweed hanging like tinsel
wet socks
soggy mattresses
we turned back
"Where are you going next?"
"I think back to Louisiana."
"Oh, ok."
I glanced at his arms

THE CHOCOLATE POODLE

open mic
at the Park Avenue Hotel
in Hot Springs

the old woman looked weary
and walked stiffly
as she arrived through the side door
with a chocolate poodle
it's eyes were fearful
tentatively scanning the room
unsure, stepping and tapping
on the marble floor
like a nervous bodyguard

they crossed the lobby
she placed the dog in the elevator
and closed an old metal gate
half the height of the elevator
we watched as she did this

she read her poem
then the Yugoslavian read a poem
about George Burns

THE FOUNTAIN

the old man
approached the hot spring water fountain
one pant leg rolled up to a knee
with bare calf exposed
his hair was a balding crew cut
and when he leaned over
he cupped the steaming water
over and over
through his palms and fingers
and washed the water
over his head
rinsing and cleansing
before drawing a plastic cup full
and drinking deeply

THE SERBIAN CLERGYMAN

antique brass fixtures
deep burgundy carpet
crystal lights

it can be awkward
riding an elevator with a stranger

this man makes no eye contact
he's a man of the 'collar'
"What church do you represent?"
a long pause
(I expect clergy to be open and friendly
this man seems cold and distant
almost annoyed)

he responds reserved and resolutely
"Serbian Orthodox!"
(I consider that there is a war in Serbia)
he proclaims with pride
and with a hint of defiance
"Serbia is a nation you know!!"

(would his attitude have been different
if he had known my great grandpa
was born in Serbia)

he steps off the elevator
and never looks back

PENNY

Penny was born blind

in Atlanta
she fell into the subway
someone jumped in and saved her
it didn't faze her
she came to Texas
and completed a Master's degree

she lived across from
her academic department
we would often see her
head tilted to one side
listening
before crossing the street

her apartment was a disaster
but there was logic to the mess
she made pathways
through the soda cans
and crumpled papers
there were paths to the bathroom
paths to the couch
paths to the kitchen
she didn't want anything moved

until her partially sighted boyfriend
planned a visit
then she asked for help

I wish she would have left those paths, though
so he could have seen just how much
of a survivor she really was

MILES TO GO

it was late and dark
the child sat terse

children need
safety
protection
security
it's a stark reminder
that sometimes it goes all wrong
when a parent stumbles
and can't get back up

with miles to go
he sang out!
"God Bless America!!"

he paused, and solemnly said,
"I prayed to Jesus someone would help me"

he paused again, and then sang,
"Jesus loves me this I know"

IT'S 4:50 AT THE DMV

it's 4:50 PM now
we pulled our numbers
and found a spot to wait at the DMV
most looked bored and tired
avoiding eye contact
but not him
he glanced around the room
seemed defensive
maybe he already knew the answer

three times
he tried to get a driver's license

"Sir, that's an old ID, it won't work."
　　"It's a military ID!!"

"I'm sorry, sir, it won't work."
　　he hovered over her
　　showing her an envelope with a
　　current address

"Sir, you need an ID, a passport . . ."
　　he showed the clerk something else
"Sir . . ."
　　　　he didn't stay to listen
　　　　he threw all his papers at her!!

as an afterthought, she yelled
"and . . . don't come back!!!"

it's 5PM at the DMV

THE DOLLAR GENERAL

standing in line at the neighborhood D.G.
six feet apart or closer

bags of kitty litter
melatonin
notebooks
guy with black tattoos fading green
Heath Bars
glancing eye contact
toilet paper
cashews
girl with piercings heavy with bling
light bulbs
small talk
and cat food
good ole' boy with a package of diapers
energy drinks
smiles
beans
and aluminum foil
giggling teens with bags of Takis

the lines for parking spaces
are worn
and barely visible

THIS DOG

the dog intimidates some neighbors
those who walk their dogs
past his house
pass with a respectful distance
and a wary glance

I like to make eye contact with this dog
he looks lonely
and sad
he just stops in his tracks
and stares at me

his owner warns everyone
not to come close

but I want to pet this dog
I want to pat his head
and gently hug his floppy ears
he knows this

CONNECTED LIKE CLOCKWORK

train whistle
in the middle of the night
connects all who hear it
together in an unseen moment in time
a whole town at that point is joined
we all share the warning
sometimes urgent
and whether we are aware
or not
multiple triggers and signals are sensed
clear and present at first
sometimes lazy
and then
as fading sensory memories
as if lost in spaces
on to the next town
connecting all
as it winds down tracks
warning, joining, connecting
like clockwork

WE ARE ONE

we are one planet
with rooms connected
by sea and salt
no one stands alone

we are connected by
air and breeze
we are together
whether recognized or not

there are no conspiracies
high like the sun
no politics
low like the moon

we are one
no disease separates us
we are one

MASKS

between groups that differ
there has been a space
class and culture
color and race
attitudes disrupt a certain balance
perceptions force us apart
interactions can be manipulated
by social power

with this new separation
comes eye contact
sometimes bold
sometimes shy
no distance can mistake
this new connection
this new exploring of a meaning
deeper than eye color

THE QUIET ZONE

seated in a quiet zone
we share the space and focus
in these places we come to listen
and feel our spirits

the quiet hum of the heat
the stir of the air above
just a chill on our feet

we prepare for a lesson
from the moment of truth
and hear the meaning
spoken in between the beats

memories
(1962 – 1971)

THE SEGREGATED TOWN

in 1962 I was eight years old
we had moved to Durant, Mississippi
a town where the schools were segregated
a year when 36 black churches
were burned down
the year the Ole Miss riot raged in Oxford
during which Paul and Ray
were murdered execution style

a white and Negro town
I walked home from school alone
carrying a lunch box
counting telephone poles
kicking rocks doing things
most kids do when they are bored

I spotted some Negro children
laughing and free and playing
near the railroad tracks
under the bridge by the creek
hopeful to join in I walked towards them
but when their mother saw me
she shoved the screen door open
and stepped out onto the worn wooden porch
looking worried and frantic and fearful
shouting to her children to
"get in the house! right now!!"

and now they looked fearful, too
and I just stood there for a moment
as she gathered them to her like baby chicks
thinking I didn't feel like a hawk or a coyote

if only she had known and understood
I had not grown up in that town

THE BAY OF PIGS

the Bay of Pigs
had been intensifying

living so close to the coast
there were air raid drills
in our elementary school

we crouched under desks
or with hands over heads
and one time under the bleachers

we waited

I imagined
that the Blue Angels
would soon fly over

NOVEMBER 1963

second row from the door
four seats back

there was something different
in the intercom "tone"
the teacher had a strained expression
she told us to be quiet
as she left the room

when she returned
we learned that my president
had been assassinated

the next day
during recess
three girls – classmates
girls I really didn't know
came to school

one dressed in red
one dressed in white
one dressed in blue

they cheered on the playground
"Kennedy is dead!!"
"Kennedy is dead!!"

I stood behind the teacher
she nervously glanced at me

I came to understand
John F. Kennedy
meant Civil Rights
　　　-the freedom for all to vote
　　　-the end to their school
　　　-the end to their way of life

RUFUS YOUNGBLOOD

in 1968 we lived next door
to Rufus Youngblood
in Vienna, Virginia
for a year

Rufus used his body
to shield Vice President Johnson
during the tragic assassination
of John Fitzgerald Kennedy
in Dallas, Texas

later President Johnson
made him the head
of the secret service

outside DC you never knew
who you might
be living next door to

I never once saw him
he simply drove his car
into his garage
and closed the door
into the deep recesses
of a confidential world

CRAZY MARTHA

crazy Martha
lived with her father
in a wind worn shack
in Hatch, New Mexico
paralleled by a dusty side road
and a barbed wire fence

he sat on the porch
in a wooden rocker
staring at us
over the brim of a dirty hat
rocking and staring
his hands gripped the rocker arms

Martha wasn't quite right
she sat behind me in second grade
and drew a picture of a stickman pee'ing
why the teacher didn't understand
I'll never know
but she paddled Martha
in front of the class

Martha came to my house after that
I had dolls
she wanted to bury one
so we buried a doll in the garden

THE BOY AND THE PARAKEET

roaming
the neighborhood
in Crocket, Texas
jumping up and down
on a stranger's trampoline

a boy showed off
as he rode his horse
acting all big and grown up
me with my fists on my hips

spying on a parakeet
through a front glass window
gazing into a home
at a small emerald bird

the woman opened the cage
to show the bird could fly
it flew furiously around the room

when she opened the screen door
it brushed by my face

the boy on the horse
pulled on the reins
and we watched
the green bird fly away

THE QUARTER

the teacher looked stern
after coming in from recess

"Who took the quarter off my desk?"
no one said anything
we all stared at the floor

she lined us up
told everyone to close their eyes
and march around the room
around the chairs
around her desk
"Whoever stole that quarter,
put it on my desk,
and you won't get in trouble."

we all marched silently
around the room
until she stopped us
but no one had returned the quarter

she lined us up again
had us turn around
and proceeded to smack each one of us
with a long wooden paddle

I still wonder who stole that quarter
do they ever think about it

RETALIATION

during recess that day
at the Sioux City
elementary school
sides were chosen
and bases taken

I covered third base
and he came
running around the bases
as fast as you please
and as he passed
he kicked me hard in the shins
with his pointy cowboy boots
grinning all the way to home base

when it was my turn
to run the bases
I kicked him hard
at third base
the same way he had kicked me
but, with soft shoes

he screamed
and held his leg
in exaggerated pain
grinning again

I got caught
and was sent back to the classroom
smug and resolved
the retaliator is the one who
usually gets caught

(best home run ever)

THE FOOTBALL

the doctor told her parents
"she needs to wear pants to school"
in 1963 girls wore dresses
"she needs to keep her legs warm"
so, I wore pants to school

somewhere on the playground
I heard the bell ring
recess was over

there it was
I picked it up
the Football

heading to the door
I held that ball like a prize
eyes locked on my teacher
and in that instance
her expression changed

and then it went dark
I was at the bottom of
a pile of boys
- tackled!!

I stood up
shook it off

stood tall
and handed the football
to the teacher

touch down!

(turns out I didn't have Juvenile RA after all)

THE GIRL'S LOCKER ROOM

the worst part of gym
was the requirement
to shower after class
shower heads dripping
and echoing from stall to stall
flip flops suctioned to the floor
the combined scent
of a dozen or so deodorants
usually no one paid attention
standing in front of your locker
dressing hurriedly

suddenly a bully
was in the quiet girl's space
"Do you hate anyone?"
sensing a trick question
the quiet girl said with
a little hesitation, "yes"
was it a lie?
doesn't everyone hate someone?
this threw the bully off
she looked confused
her answer had been rehearsed
so, she went ahead and said it
"Well, I hate people who don't hate anyone."

FALLING ROCKS

highway signs warn
"watch for falling rocks"

that always caught my attention
perking up
standing
on the floorboard of the car
watching
as we approached the cliffs
were beside the cliffs
and after the cliffs
always disappointed
that I never saw them fall

has anyone ever seen them fall
maybe when you least expect it

BOEING 747

In January 1970
Pat Nixon christened
the Pan Am Boeing 747
at Dulles International Airport
with red, white, and blue water
instead of champagne

a massive plane
it flew low
over our Virginia suburb
almost as if it was suspended in air
and as if it could
just gently
float to the ground somehow

NIXON

some of us went into DC to sightsee
we explored the Capitol building
the subway under the dome
walked to the White House
rounded a corner

the black, wrought iron gates
of the side entrance
made a slight groaning sound
deliberately opening slowly
and as they opened
a long black limousine
edged out cautiously

President Richard Nixon
only a few feet away
looked directly at me
his expression was strained
worried
behind the thick glass window
he seemed small
and unsure
when he waved

staying
centered

MOON'S GLOW

ethereal has a meaning
that floats into your soul
and finds moments
to play with air

no boundaries
moon's glow
without density
expanding into new limits
where space
is the dark side of light

ZEPHYR

time slipped past midnight
I heard the seconds as they paused
the chilly rain as it drowned
and deeper, deeper down
drops like black ink soak the ground
obscuring light, the dark, no star
a zephyr leaves a trail
revealing nature's icy cause
and leaving most sky's pale
gone are meadows green
and all the leaves entailed
blustery blue air, frozen streams
and frosted fields, the cold prevails
it snowed then
so many flakes, so wild and free
in mounds buried deep, deep, deep
the air so stirred shrouds every tree
the crispness on the ground it lay
all surface found, no shape to keep
the snow it fell, it lulled to sleep
so clean, so clear, I think it may
portray no sound this winter day

A CALM SOUL

could I calm my soul today
restless to wander
the distant way

a certain serenity
lasts for a time
if bound by a tranquil smile

could I calm my soul
cause it to be so still
like a winter snow fall

SPATIAL LAPSE

today stops in pauses
the air is still
thoughts perceive the synapse
crossing a spatial lapse
there are no meanings in a light
that flashes instantly
as if a point was reached
to save its place in time

THE SPEED OF LIGHT

sensitivity is increasing my perception
the incentive is not hidden
just dormant
as a still pause in a double standard
I then explore
the vastness of inspiration
illuminated 186,000 miles into space

CONTINUOUS FLOW

pausing for a moment
sensing
that the eternal ripples
have their say

it seems everlasting
you realize
here is something
never ending
each minute wave
lasting for a second
only to be joined
in the continuous
flow of matter

PERSPECTIVE

perspective gains it's meaning
when waves
abound in light
the ceaseless
tossing rolling surge
of ocean's salty plight

a cycle that
the moon and clouds
reveal each day
each night
along the coast
along the world
a long and endless sight

MOIRAI

a pink dawn lingers
as she makes her way to the beach
tracing feather-like patterns of mice and snails
in the wet sand with her toes
wind blows over the ocean waves
pausing long enough to become aware
of the warm water washing
first her ankles
then her knees
her feet reach for something solid underneath
with each wave she perceives a certain balance
and with each wave
more and more space washes away beneath her
her arms float
as if suspended by strings
threads attached to soft stars
sea gulls circle with their curious heads
cocked to the side
soon they could be tangled in her floating hair
the distant horizon is dark violet
she breathes deeply of the salty air
and tastes the ocean

the shore becomes a life path
and she follows

SEA WIND

high water marks
have leveled the sand ridges
wet dust
salty dead sea smells
capture my perception
as clamoring sea gulls
attack the frothy waves

I remain standing
while the ocean
laps my ankles
and fresh sea wind
unravels my hair

CIRCLES

when the lines of my circle
eventually met
I realized that circumference was superficial
and that many more lines in circles
must meet
before even completing something
which speaks form
and my life is no longer
just circles because of that

PROGRESSION

realization of self
dawns slowly
just as a sunrise
announces its arrival gradually
one senses a change in self
must be gradual
a progression
becoming a portion
of the more complete one

PEN TO PAPER

this poetry is something
with which
I hope to regain time
for into past securities
the sounds jump up to rhyme
their lessons are the frail birds
vast legions of them heard
and from my pen to paper
I extricate their words

A POEM APPEARS

I grow a little conscious
of what these phrases bring
fragmented
sometimes rigid
so peculiar they do seem
a little dash
apostrophes
a comma
here and there
syntax and some pentameter
a verse
a poem appears

IN YOUR SOUL

mystical insights
remain connected
to the notes of language
illuminating gray shadows

you reflect
in the ocean's white sand
and the moon's blue light
and in your soul
remains the same

FOR RICHARD

somewhere his colors appeared
and he struggled
past the black and white fields

into late nights at the print lab
new resistance was structured
now around the planes which
spring from generalities
and bright favorites are patterned
in controlled areas of surface

so goes the transition

SUPPOSE

suppose we wade into the sky
of blue and white and sail up high
suppose we fade out to the clear
and scale the flight not distant – near

suppose the land sinks out of sight
and opens up a way
its then I'll see you on the edge
perhaps you'll see me dear

CLOSE TO ME

beyond the still remembrance
of feelings unexplained
locked within a sigh
alive and so untamed
some call it passion unashamed
some call it sweet and free
but in my mind's solution
I call it close to me

QUINTESSENCE

the green, green earth orbits and spins
in unison with the ocean's tides
pausing for a moment, perceiving
that the wide rolling waves are boundless
each ripple absorbed by a fathomless blue
tossing, bubbling, and surging
a progression connecting balmy breeze
and water, body and soul, ebb, and flow
sand can lie silent and still
but with pressure from the ever-pounding surf
granules may form a mold
a temporary work of art, a soft inlay, a subtle slope
winds and waves press on all day
and play their role in this display
we need the ocean and wind and sand
to teach us and shape us
we are separate, but we are one planet
in rooms connected by salt and sea

WATCHING THE STARS

late night decaf
stirred sweet with a fork
cooled
swirled
and bubbling air
below the surface
no cold steps
just an open window
enough to breathe
and for
cat
to watch the stars

VINES

whispering syllables
remind me of cautious secrets
where words lack dimension
and darken
what lies behind the eyes

when actions are disguised
in symbolic interactions
tangled in a system of reasons
that don't rhyme
like vines clinging inside minds
with inconsistent timing
for the many who had
to endure a divergent walk
when gravity denied an exit

MISPLACED CARES

cares are misplaced
and forgotten
in the cavity
of an uncertain mind
where words somehow
lack the balance
needed to provoke thoughts
and opinions
in order
to scatter clouds of inhumanity

a humanity that won't stir in unison
unlike formations of geese
focused on
travelling strong
in a symbolic formation
destined to
find remembered spaces

ORDER

order is predicted
in some lives
when tomatoes
are arranged like pyramids
in local supermarkets
waiting for that one tomato
to be pulled
sparking a cascade
of red boulders
sliding toward
the apples
the avocados
and the pears
that moment of truth
(most likely being watched
by security cameras
capturing the anxiety)
carefully arranging it all
once again
thinking maybe this
might actually
be a good place to work

HIJINKS

liberated minutes
and unconfined lies
line hours of spoken conversation
in a back and forth hijinks
cascading into wild labels
opening discourse between
revealers of truth for not giving
into fables that confuse
and refuse to lower frustration
feeding into the gaps
and not refuting
the tags and tickets
lost to jazz and sweet tea
compositions inside
the balconies of minds
tearing notes to break free
and letting the mystic beats
and notes
rise beyond occasions
and beyond time

DOES IT MATTER

history in syllables
and consonants
typed and stored
boxed and taped
and shredded
like evidence lost
to the future
marking time no more
receipts showing
when and where you
were for days and weeks
marking your place
does it matter
letting it all go

FINALLY

in the cellular places
where feelings compete
with concerns that shouldn't rhyme
where imaginary words
attempt to seep
out of pores
and pretend they can think
on their own
when random papers
caught by breezes
collect in tree hollows
where they collude
and work their way
into some type of meaning
some type of plan
where something
finally makes sense

EMILY

what do we really know about Emily
she thrived on listening to the world's heartbeat
from within a room with one window

where did the insight come from

she knew without knowing
the questions to ask
the questions future generations
would continue to ponder
year after day after life

she heard a fly buzz when she died

that buzzing frequency that carried her soul
away from a fading sensorial world
to a spaceless time where all words coalesce

THE FRAGRANCE OF MEMORY

I missed the sunset tonight
but was able to recall
a fragrant peach
from the past
and settle into a quiet observance
of a secret sun
where bright noisy sounds
evaporate into the lingering light

Brenda Linkeman began writing poetry when she was a sophomore in high school and only recently began publishing. She has had poems published in The *Gasconade Review* and the *Trailer Park Quarterly.* She has made a career working as a clinical social worker and play therapist with children, as well as teaching private art lessons. Brenda grew up moving frequently since her father was a topographic engineer for the USGS. She has lived in seventeen states. Living all over the U.S. allowed her to learn about the variety of landscapes in this country, and the often subtle, but unique cultural differences there are between the states. The dynamics between people inspires Brenda's poetry, as does the universe.

This project was made possible, in part, by generous support from the Osage Arts Community.

Osage Arts Community provides temporary time, space and support for the creation of new artistic works in a retreat format, serving creative people of all kinds — visual artists, composers, poets, fiction and nonfiction writers. Located on a 152-acre farm in an isolated rural mountainside setting in Central Missouri and bordered by ¾ of a mile of the Gasconade River, OAC provides residencies to those working alone, as well as welcoming collaborative teams, offering living space and workspace in a country environment to emerging and mid-career artists. For more information, visit us at www.osageac.org

Osage Arts Community